THE WIND
WHISPERS
WARNING

Lowell Lundstrom

THE WIND WHISPERS WARNING

Lowell Lundstrom Ministries, Inc.
Sisseton, South Dakota 57262

The Wind Whispers Warning

Copyright © 1979
Lowell Lundstrom Ministries, Inc.
Sisseton, South Dakota 57262
ISBN 0-938220-13-6

Additional copies of this book are available for $1.95 each. Special price available for larger quantities.

Order additional copies by writing:
Lowell Lundstrom Ministries, Inc.
Sisseton, South Dakota 57262

First printing, July 1979—10,000
Second printing, February 1980—10,000
Third printing, October 1980—10,000

Contents

Foreword

Great winds of change are blowing over Earth.

In recent months the United States has granted diplomatic recognition to Red China. This is a desperate effort to bolster our economy by increasing exports. The United States is also seeking to stop Russian expansion by allying with Red China.

Russia is making bold moves to take over the world, especially the Mideast which has the oil to keep Western industry running. If Russia can choke off the oil supply or cause the price of oil to rise dramatically,

she believes the Western nations will go to their knees.

The Shah has been thrown out of Iran; and the leftist, communist organizations are working to overthrow the present Iranian government. One thing is certain from Bible prophecy: the nation of Iran will ally with Russia when the Russians invade Israel.

Israel is in possession of the Holy City, Jerusalem. Jesus said when we see Jerusalem in the hands of the Jewish nation we are living in the last days.

Not only are the winds of political change blowing everywhere, the wind of the Holy Spirit is blowing—whispering warning to Christians and non-Christians, telling them to prepare for the soon return of Jesus Christ.

The apostle John wrote in his letter, *"...it is the last time: and as ye have heard that antichrist shall come, even now are there many antichrists; whereby we know that it is the last time. They went out from us, but they were not of us; for if they had been of us, they would no doubt have continued with us: but they went out, that they might be made mani-*

fest that they were not all of us. But ye have an unction from the Holy One, and ye know all things" (1 John 2:18-20). If we will heed the wind of the Holy Spirit, if we will respond to the *"unction from the Holy One,"* we will not be caught unprepared.

God's Word and the Holy Spirit enable us *to know all things.* The chapters of this book were born of the Holy Spirit. I never planned to write a book until this series of messages began to burn in my heart. I am certain you will find the great prophecies being fulfilled in our day a great revelation of the truth of the Scriptures.

ONE

The Dragon Comes to Supper!

The United States is playing a dangerous but necessary game. The communist governments of China and Russia are determined to destroy democracy throughout the world—and now the U.S. has granted diplomatic recognition to China as Canada did years ago.

This will enable China to purchase the technology she needs to become a super military power. U.S. corporations are looking forward to billions of dollars in business. But there's more than business at stake. Dr. C. M. Ward, a specialist in Bible prophecy, said, "The present situation will leave Russia checkmated in her ambition for world conquest. World power is in the balance. Look for the United

States to build a huge air base in the Sinai Peninsula to protect the Arab oil nations. Russia is posing an economic threat to Japan by moving toward Mideast oil. (Japan gets 90 percent of her oil from the Mideast.) Japan is looking to China for help. Keep in mind that if you take off the first two letters of "spoil" you have "oil."

The danger of the U.S. move in giving diplomatic recognition and technology to China is that, politically, America is playing two enemies against each other, trying to buy time and tip the scale in the balance of power.

Russia may be checkmated for now but not for long. What will happen if Russia and China resolve their differences? The bear and dragon will devour the West.

We are moving into the last days when, Jesus said, "...There shall be (...) upon the earth distress of nations...men's hearts failing them for fear, and for looking after those things which are coming on the earth..." *(cf. Luke 21:23-26)*.

I believe the technology the Chinese will receive from new trade agreements with the United States and Japan will help modernize her army, which is estimated at more than two million strong! China not only has a super population (nearly one billion), she is going to be a super power! Western technology will prepare China for the end-time battle known as Armageddon.

The dictionary says Armageddon is a "place of final conflict between the forces of good and evil."

In Revelation, chapter 16, you can read about the last-day judgments God will pour out upon the Earth. Despite the severity of these judgments, the inhabitants of the world will not change their minds about God, nor will they turn from evil. The Bible says, *"...(They) blasphemed the God of heaven because of their pains and their sores, and repented not of their deeds" (Revelation 16:11).*

Notice the reference to China in the following verse: *"And the sixth angel poured out his vial upon the great river Euphrates; and the water thereof was dried up, that the way of the kings of the east might be prepared" (Revelation 16:12).* The kings of the east represent a confederacy of powers located east of Israel (Japan may be included).

Hal Lindsay, in his book, *The Late Great Planet Earth,* points out that the original Greek word translated "east" in the Scriptures is, literally, "anatolesheliou" which means "the rising of the sun." "Anatolesheliou" was the ancient designation of the Oriental race. John describes the vast horde of soldiers assembled at the Euphrates River as the "kings of the sun rising" and so definitely predicts the movements of an Oriental army into war in the Mideast.

The Euphrates is also significant. For centuries this 1800-mile-long river has been a boundary between the peoples of the East and those of the West. This boundary also points to the fact that the powers mentioned in Revelation 16:12 are Oriental: "the kings of the sun rising" are to come from the eastern side of the Euphrates River.

John continues in Revelation 16: *"And I saw three unclean spirits like frogs come out of the mouth of the dragon, and out of the mouth of the beast (the anti-Christ), and out of the mouth of the false prophet.*

"For they are the spirits of devils, working miracles, which go forth unto the kings of the earth and of the whole world, to gather them to the battle of that great day of God Almighty." Verse 16 records, *"...he gathered*

them together into a place called in the Hebrew tongue Armageddon."

China is headed for the last great battle of the nations described in Revelation, chapter 19. We can see from this scripture that the dragon will come for supper, the supper of the great God. God will call the vultures of heaven to clean up the carnage of the dragon's remains.

Diplomatic recognition of China by the U.S., however, may also result in unexpected freedom for the church. Since World War II, the Bamboo Curtain has been closed to Christian missionary activity just as the Russian Iron Curtain has tried to shut out the church. Many feared it was "curtains" for world evangelism, but God has been doing a great thing in opening impossible doors throughout the world. The Holy Spirit has been moving in the U.S.S.R., and the church has been growing despite persecution.

Now China watchers predict that China will allow more freedom of Christian activity if for no other reason than to impress the West. If the Chinese government does allow more religious freedom, many Chinese will come to know Jesus Christ as their Savior and, as a result, will join Him and the saints from all the ages in what is known as the Marriage Supper of the Lamb *(cf. Revelation 19:9)*.

The Gospel seed has been sown in China through the Far East Broadcasting Company and the one-million-watt radio station in Taiwan. These powerful stations have been beaming the Gospel into China for nearly three decades.

I believe a harvest is coming.

Two things have happened to prepare China for a great spiritual awakening: the communist government has eradicated idolatry, and Mandarin has become the official language, uniting this vast country.

Missionaries, by faith, have prepared themselves in the Mandarin Chinese language and have published materials ready for the moment permission is granted for them to evangelize. So, while world governments are rushing toward Armageddon, the Holy Spirit is moving to bring about one last great spiritual harvest.

Jesus said, "I will build my church" *(cf. Matthew 16:18)*. Even now the church is rediscovering the power and glory it had in the first century when it "turned the world upside down." Even though things look dark for the world, the future has never looked brighter for God's people. The closer we are to the end, the nearer we are to the great marriage supper of the Lamb: *"...Blessed (Happy) are they which are called unto the marriage supper of the Lamb..." (Revelation 19:9).*

As we are living in the last days, keep these things in mind. First, spend more time in Bible reading and prayer: *"...take heed to your-selves lest your hearts be weighed down with dissipation and drunkenness and cares of this life, and that day come upon you suddenly like a snare; for it will come upon all who dwell upon the face of the whole earth. But watch at all times, praying that you may have strength to escape all these things that will take place, and to stand before the Son of man" (Luke 21:24-36).*

Second, build your marriage and home with family devotions. Third, walk in the Spirit so you will have the strength to resist seducing spirits of immorality and evil: *"Now the Spirit speaketh expressly, that in the latter times some shall depart from the faith, giving heed to seducing spirits, and doctrines of devils" (1 Timothy 4:1).* Most of all, *"Let your light so shine before men, that they may see your good works, and glorify your Father which is in heaven"(Matthew 5:16).*

We are coming down to the wire! Keep your soul on fire for the day of the Lord is at hand! Remember, the dragon is coming for supper.

TWO

Bear Tracks in the Sand!

Something serious is happening to the world balance of power. In recent years many Mideast countries that were once allied with the West have fallen under the influence of Marxism and are now within the Russian orbit of influence.

There are bear tracks all over the sands of the Mideast.

Newsweek Magazine recently reported that when Saudi Ambassador, Ali Alireza, met with a group of dignitaries in Washington, honoring the departing Pakistani envoy, Alireza stunned his guests by sounding an alarm about Soviet designs in the Red Sea, the Arabian Peninsula and the Persian Gulf.

Alireza declared, "Our friends (which include the United States and Canada), do not seem to realize that a crisis of historic magnitude is close at hand for the Western world, and for those who share its values in our entire area."

Responding to Alireza, Yaqub Khan, the Pakistani envoy, went even further to say, "I fear that historians will look back at 1978 as a watershed year, when the balance of power shifted against the Western world." In regard to the shift of power, the Pakistani Ambassador is being transferred from Washington to Moscow with specific instructions to establish closer ties with Russia.

There are a growing number of Russian bear tracks in the dry desert sands of these countries which were once allies of the West. This shift of nations is tilting the balance of power in favor of the Russians.

In the last 20 years, many nations have switched their allegiance. Libya, once the location of one of the largest airbases of the Western Alliance but now in the hands of the radical Kadaffi, is no longer an ally of democracy.

The Sudan has become a military dictatorship, no longer pro-Western in policy.

Ethiopia has become a Russian power base for all of Africa.

In Southern Yemen the Soviets have organized an international communist brigade.

Afghanistan is now a Soviet protectorate, another base of power for the Russians.

Iraq is a militant, anti-Western country.

Syria has been allied with the Russian plans for destruction of Israel for many years.

Recently we have been hearing about the Shah and turmoil in Iran. According to Bible prophecy, Iran will end up within the Russian sphere of influence (*cf. Ezekiel 38:5*).

Newsweek Magazine reports, "The Saudis charge that Soviet agents have been subverting Iran's regime at the same time that Moscow has been telling Western officials that it is afraid of the chaos that might follow the Shah's fall."

For many years Bible scholars have known what will happen in the Mideast because of the prophecies Ezekiel was given in the Book of Ezekiel, chapters 37, 38 and 39.

The Bible says, "...*Thus saith the Lord God; Behold, I will take the children of Israel from among the heathen, whither they be gone, and will gather them on every side, and bring them into their own land: And I will make them one nation in the land upon the mountains of Israel" (Ezekiel 37:21,22a).*

This scripture, along with many others, reveals that in the last days God would gather Israel and make her a nation again. This prophecy was fulfilled 30 years ago, and since that time we have been living in what prophetic scripture calls the last days.

Ezekiel 37:25 says, *"And they shall dwell in the land that I have given unto Jacob my servant...forever...."* We know from Bible prophecy that Israel will never be destroyed. God says the land is Israel's permanent inheritance!

Chapter 38 reveals what will happen when the Russian bear and her allies launch an invasion of Israel: *"And the word of the Lord came unto me, saying, Son of man, set thy face against Gog, the land of Magog, the chief prince of Meshech and Tubal, and prophesy against him, And say, Thus saith the Lord God; Behold, I am against thee, O Gog, the chief prince of Meshech and Tubal..." (Ezekiel 38:1-3).*

To understand who the prophet is speaking

of it is necessary for you to go to a Bible map depicting this region at the time that Ezekiel prophesied. Geographers and Bible scholars are unanimous in agreeing that Gog, the land of Magog, refers to the land located north of Israel. Today it is called Russia.

Verse 15 of chapter 38 proves this: *"And thou shalt come from thy place out of the north parts...."* If you take a globe of the world, locate Israel, then move your finger north and you will find Russia.

The Bible says, *"And I will turn thee back, and put hooks into thy jaws, and I will bring thee forth, and all thine army, horses and horsemen, all of them clothed with all sorts of armour, even a great company with bucklers and shields, all of them handling swords..."* *(Ezekiel 38:4).*

If the prophet's description sounds outdated, remember that Ezekiel never saw a modern tank or a machine gun. The only way Ezekiel could describe modern weapons was in the imagery he understood, *"...Horses... clothed with all sorts of armour, even a great company...handling swords...."*

Then the prophet lists the nations that will join Russia in her invasion of Israel. The first nation mentioned is Persia. This country is known today as Iran. For 18 years I have been saying, based on Bible prophecy, that Iran, one of the West's staunchest allies, would one day end up with the Russians in their war against Israel. The turmoil in Iran today shows that Iran will be controlled by the Russians as they move into other countries of the area.

The Bible continues, "...*Persia, Ethiopia, and Libya with them; all of them with shield and helmet* (It almost sounds like a repetition of what I mentioned earlier in the shift of alliances): *Gomer, and all his bands* (This refers to East Germany); *the house of Togarmah* (known today as Southern Russia) *of the north quarters, and all his bands: and many people with thee*" (*Ezekiel 38:5,6*).

Then the Bible describes the battle between the bear and her allies against Israel: "*After many days thou shalt be visited: in the latter years thou shalt come* (speaking of Russia) *into the land that is brought back from the sword, and is gathered out of many people* (Remember, Israel was gathered out of all of the nations of the world, and the United Nations voted in 1947 to make Palestine a homeland for the Jews, fulfilling this prophecy), *against the mountains of Israel, which have been always waste: but it is brought forth out of the nations, and they shall dwell safely all of them. Thou shalt ascend and come like a storm* (This language tells there will be aircraft involved in the warfare), *thou shalt be like a cloud to cover the land, thou, and all thy bands, and many people with thee."* Who will be Israel's allies? Verse 13 of Ezekiel 38 says, *"Sheba, and Dedan, and the merchants of Tarshish, with all the young lions thereof, shall say unto thee, Art thou come to take a spoil? hast thou gathered thy company to take a prey? to carry away silver and gold, to take away cattle and goods, to take a great spoil?"* In other words, the nations of the West, knowing that Israel's destruction would give Russia control of Mideast oil, knowing that Russia could shut down the entire industry of the Western world, will say to Russia, "What do you think you are trying to get away with?"

The nations that will stand with Israel against a Russian take-over of the Mideast oil fields will be Sheba and Dedan (the land known today as Saudi Arabia). The Saudis have been staunchly anti-Communist and will stand with the Israelis against the Russians.

The Bible also mentions "the merchants of Tarshish, with all the young lions thereof...." Tarshish was a prosperous seaport, and some Bible scholars believe this may refer to the modern-day Tarshish—Great Britain and her allies, referred to as the "young lions." Whatever "merchants of Tarshish" refers to, we know it has to be a great trade organization such as the Common Market or a group of Western nations like NATO with a stake in Mideast oil.

One thing is certain, many nations will come to Israel's defense, but I doubt that they will do any fighting. The reason God has called them to this land is to witness the miraculous deliverance of Israel from the Russian bear.

The Bible says, *"And it shall come to pass at the same time when Gog shall come against the land of Israel, saith the Lord God, that my fury shall come up in my face. For in my jealousy and in the fire of my wrath have I spoken, Surely in that day there shall be a great shaking in the land of Israel; so that the fishes of the sea, and the fowls of the heaven, and the beasts of the field, and all creeping things that creep upon the earth, and all the men that are upon the face of the earth, shall shake at my presence, and the mountains shall be thrown down, and the steep places shall fall, and every wall shall fall to the ground"* (Ezekiel 38:18-20).

It appears from these scriptures that God is going to cause a great earthquake that will level many of the mountains in Israel and destroy a large portion of the Russian army. This earthquake will be of such dimension that it will shake the Richter scales throughout the world; in fact, men everywhere will tremble.

"And I will call for a sword against him throughout all my mountains, saith the Lord God: every man's sword shall be against his brother. And I will plead against him with pestilence and with blood; and I will rain upon him, and upon his bands, and upon the many people that are with him, an overflowing rain, and great hailstones, fire and brimstone. Thus will I magnify myself, and sanctify myself: and I will be known in the eyes of many nations, and they shall know that I am the Lord" (Ezekiel 38:21-23).

Now the Lord God is called "the Lion of the tribe of Judah," and it is going to be an awesome moment when the Lion of Judah takes on the Russian bear!

Chapter 39 of Ezekiel shows that five sixths of the Russian army will be destroyed, and all of the nations will glorify God, who delivered Israel. This is why I do not believe that the nations that gather for Israel's defense will fight—because if they had won the victory themselves, they would not have given the glory to God.

The Russian bear is leaving tracks all over the sands of the Mideast, and the final alignment of nations is taking place for the showdown.

On June 8 last year, Alexander Solzhenitsyn, the Soviet exile and modern-day prophet to the West, rose to accept an honorary doctorate from Harvard. He warned the West in these words, "The fight for our planet, physical and spiritual, a fight of cosmic proportions, is not a vague matter of the future; it has already started. The forces of evil have begun their decisive offensive. You can feel their pressure, and yet your screens and publications are full of prescribed smiles and raised glasses. What is the joy about?"

Christian friend, I believe now is the time to pray and prepare our hearts for the coming of the Lord. Dangerous days are upon us, and it is time to pray more than ever. It is time to let our light shine, to witness to our friends, to share the news of what is really happening in the world today.

Make certain that your heart is right with God so that you can work for Him now. We do not have much time left. The bear is making tracks all over the Mideast. She is preparing to pounce on Israel. Jesus said, *"And when these things begin to come to pass, then look up, and lift up your heads; for your redemption draweth nigh"* (Luke 21:28).

Remember, the Russian bear tracks in the sands are foretold in God's Word, and it tells us to prepare for the coming of the Lord.

THREE

The Beast in the Blanket!

Our planet is in great peril! Did you realize that nations of the world are spending more than $368 billion a year on armaments? This amounts to more than $1 billion a day each day of the year. According to Senator Mark Hatfield of Oregon, there is enough fire power stockpiled in nuclear bombs, rockets and ammunition to equal 15 tons of dynamite per person on the face of the globe.

The Club of Rome is an elite group of world leaders who periodically meet to review the world situation. Recently they released a report entitled "Mankind at the Crossroads." The document stated, "Suddenly, virtually overnight, when measured on an historical scale, mankind finds itself confronted by a multitude of unprecedented crises: 1st, the population crisis; 2nd, the environmental crisis; 3rd, the world food crisis; 4th, the energy crisis; and 5th, the raw materials crisis—to name just a few." The report concludes, "The only alternatives *without a global plan* are division and conflict, hate and destruction."

The United Nations Secretary General has declared, "I do not wish to seem overdramatic, but I can only conclude from the information that is available to me as secretary general that the members of the United Nations have perhaps 10 years left in which to subordinate their ancient quarrels and launch a global partnership to curb the arms race, to improve the human environment, to de-fuse the population explosion, and to supply the required momentum to world development efforts." The alternative is a situation *"beyond our capacity to control."* The perilous position of our planet has leaders of the world talking about a new world government that will guarantee peace at any price.

A Princeton professor published a comprehensive work on the arms race entitled "Thinking About the Unthinkable." He said,

"The only way to solve the problem is maybe some form of world government."

The threat of nuclear war is so great that five nuclear arms experts at Harvard University and the Massachusetts Institute of Technology recently warned, "A very nasty kind of world government may be the only way to keep the world from blowing itself up in a nuclear war."

In 1860, the French scientist, Pierre Berchelt, stated that "inside of one hundred years of physical and chemical science, man will know what the atom is. It is my belief that when science reaches this stage, God will come down to Earth with His big ring of keys and will say to humanity, 'Gentlemen, it's closing time.'"

In Matthew, Jesus Christ gave us information indicating that we are in the last days: *"And this gospel of the kingdom shall be preached in all the world for a witness unto all nations; and then shall the end come"* (Matthew 24:14). If there were no other prophecy in the Bible, this prophecy alone would tell us where the world is on God's timetable. Within our generation the Christian message has gone around the world—now we can look for the end of the age! In the following verses, Jesus makes an unusual reference to the prophecies of Daniel: *"When ye therefore shall see the abomination of desolation, spoken of by Daniel the prophet, stand in the holy place, (whoso readeth, let him understand:) then let them which be in Judea flee into the mountains: let him which is on the house top not come down to take any thing out of his house: neither let him which is in the field return back to take his clothes. And woe unto them that are with child, and to them that give suck in those days! But pray ye that your flight be not in the winter, neither on the Sabbath day: for then shall be great tribulation, such as was not since the beginning of the world to this time, no, nor ever shall be. And except those days should be shortened, there should no flesh be saved: but for the elect's sake those days shall be shortened"* (Matthew 24:15-22).

When skeptics used to read the prophecy of Jesus Christ describing a coming world holocaust that would destroy nearly everyone on earth, they snickered—but they are not laughing anymore. These are dangerous days! With global powers spending $1 billion a day on arms, a population crisis, food crisis, energy crisis and a raw materials crisis, leaders are beginning to call for a world organization to bring peace to earth.

Jesus made reference to something called "the abomination of desolation" in Matthew 24:15. This reference is a key to what will happen. An individual, described as a beast, will rise to power. He will be the personification of evil. He will promise peace and prosperity and will win the favor of world governments; but after he has consolidated his position, he will embark on a reign of terror worse than the world has ever experienced. The world is yearning for security. A picture comes to my mind of the little boy who clutched his blanket whenever he was nervous or startled. Later, as an adolescent, he faced danger with the same response, "Mommy, Mommy—my blanket, blanket!" The world is crying, "Blanket, blanket!" and the Bible says the Antichrist will offer it the blanket of peace; but he will be a beast in a blanket, a satanically possessed man who will bring the world to ruin.

The prophet Daniel describes him: "...*The fourth beast shall be the fourth kingdom upon earth, which shall be diverse from all kingdoms, and shall devour the whole earth,*

and shall tread it down, and break it in pieces"
(Daniel 7:23). "And he shall speak great
words against the most High, and shall wear
out the saints of the most High..." (Daniel
7:25a). "Yea, he magnified himself even to
the prince of the host, and by him the daily
sacrifice was taken away..." (Daniel 8:11a).

"And in the latter time of their kingdom,
when the transgressors are come to the full, a
king of fierce countenance, and understanding dark sentences, shall stand up. And his
power shall be mighty, but not by his own
power: and he shall destroy wonderfully, and
shall prosper, and practice, and shall destroy
the mighty and the holy people. And through
his policy also he shall cause craft to prosper in
his hand; and he shall magnify himself in his
heart, and by peace shall destroy many: he
shall also stand up against the Prince of
princes; but he shall be broken without hand"
(Daniel 8:23-25).

"And he shall confirm the covenant with
many for one week: and in the midst of the
week he shall cause the sacrifice and the obla-
tion to cease, and for the overspreading of
abominations he shall make it desolate, even
until the consummation, and that determined

shall be poured upon the desolate" (Daniel 9:27). The beast, the Antichrist, will deceive the world, including the nation of Israel, and cause the "abomination of desolation." He will set himself up in the temple in Jerusalem as though he were Almighty God *(cf. 2 Thessalonians 2:4)*. According to Bible prophecy, that temple will soon be rebuilt. Daily religious sacrifices will be renewed, the Antichrist will establish a peaceful relationship with the Jews, and it will appear that at last an Arab-Israeli settlement has been achieved. These happenings will take place during a seven-year period, the seventieth week of Daniel (This week meaning seven years is referred to in Daniel 9:27).

In the middle of the week, or after three and one-half years, the Antichrist will break his treaty with Israel; he will bring the daily sacrifices to an end, and he will set himself up in the temple in Jerusalem as God. This act will fulfill the prophecy of the "abomination of desolation" *(cf. Matthew 24:15)*. He will throw away the blanket hiding his beastly form and will devour the world.

Consider what the apostle Paul says about the end-time deceiver: *"The coming of the lawless one by the activity of Satan will be with all power and with pretended signs and wonders, and with all wicked deception for those who are to perish, because they refused to love the truth and so be saved. Therefore God sends upon them a strong delusion, to make them believe what is false, so that all may be condemned who did not believe the truth but had pleasure in unrighteousness" (2 Thessalonians 2:9-12, RSV).*

The world will be deceived by the beast in the blanket because the world turned from the truth. When a man refuses to believe the Word of God, he will be deceived by Satan. Jesus said, *"...I am the way, the truth, and the life: no man cometh unto the Father, but by me" (John 14:6).* Before the beast's reign of terror upon earth, those who have prepared themselves for Christ's return will be caught away to be with Him.

The last days are upon us. World leaders are seeking for one great man to obtain and preserve global peace; and the Antichrist, the beast in the blanket, will appear and deceive the world.

William Blake said, "A truth that's told with bad intent beats all (the) lies you can invent."

The world needs peace, but the world will not turn to Jesus Christ, the Prince of peace. Christian friends, we must prepare for our Lord's return. I hope that if you are serving Him, you will share your testimony with as many people as you can. If you are not serving Him as you should, pray to make things right with Him. Now is the time to look up—He is coming: *"...when these things begin to come to pass, then look up, and lift up your heads; for your redemption draweth nigh"* (Luke 21:28).

FOUR

The Kingdom of the Beast!

A scholar, who studied Bible prophecy for more than forty years, was asked what he thought of present-day developments. He said, "I think we are at the brink!"

The Russian bear and the Chinese dragon have been maneuvering for positions of power on the political chessboard of the world, but the Bible says a man—more fierce and powerful than they—will take over! The Bible calls him the beast. He is described in Revelation, chapter 13: *"And I stood upon the sand of the sea, and saw a beast rise up out of the sea, having seven heads and ten horns, and upon his horns ten crowns, and upon his heads the name of blasphemy" (Revelation 13:1).*

If the description of a beast rising out of the sea puzzles you, remember that scripture always interprets scripture. Isaiah 57:20,21 records that *"...the wicked are like the troubled sea, when it cannot rest, whose waters cast up mire and dirt. There is no peace, saith my God, to the wicked."* The sea that John the apostle is speaking about in Revelation 13:1 is the sea of humanity out of which rises the terrible beast.

The Bible says, *"...the beast which I saw was like unto a leopard, and his feet were as the feet of a bear, and his mouth as the mouth of a lion..." (Revelation 13:2a).* This coming world leader will move with the swiftness of a leopard, the strength of a bear and will have the all-consuming appetite of a lion.

Verse 2 of Revelation 13 continues, *"...and the dragon gave him his power, and his seat, and great authority."* Who is the dragon that will give the beast his authority? Verse 9 of the preceding chapter tells us: *"...the great dragon was cast out, that old serpent, called the Devil, and Satan, which deceiveth the whole world...."* The devil gives the Antichrist the power he needs to become the worldwide dictator.

As mentioned in chapter 3, world leaders realize that to preserve the human race from thermonuclear destruction, there must be a new world government under the direction of a dictator. Arnold Toynbee, one of the greatest historians of all time, said, "One of the most conspicuous marks of a disintegrating society is when it purchases a reprieve by submitting to forcible, political unification." Hal Lindsay says in his book, *The Terminal Generation*, "A world that is terrified at the thought of war will welcome with open arms and relieved sighs the Antichrist and his magnanimous leadership."

Verse 3 of Revelation, chapter 13, continues its description of the Antichrist: *"And I saw one of his heads as it were wounded to death; and his deadly wound was healed: and all the world wondered after the beast."* Apparently the coming world dictator will suffer what will seem to be death and then experience satanic resurrection.

Just as Christ's resurrection by the power of God shook the world in the first century, so what appears to be a resurrection of the Antichrist will shake the world in the last days. His recovery will cause the world to marvel at the

41

messiah of madness.

The Bible says, *"they worshipped the dragon which gave power unto the beast* (i.e., they worshiped the devil): *and they worshipped the beast, saying, Who is like unto the beast? who is able to make war with him" (Revelation 13:4).* The power of this devilish dictator will be overwhelming!

"And there was given unto him a mouth speaking great things and blasphemies; and power was given unto him to continue forty and two months" (Revelation 13:5). The Antichrist will rule the world for three and one-half years; his reign will end when Jesus returns to the earth to set up His everlasting Kingdom.

"And it was given unto (the beast) to make war with the saints, and to overcome them: and power was given him over all kindreds, and tongues, and nations. And all that dwell upon the earth shall worship him, whose names are not written in the book of life of the Lamb slain from the foundation of the world" (Revelation 13:7,8). This verse clearly declares that the Antichrist will have ultimate power over everyone living on earth. No one will be able to escape his sphere of influence.

The Bible mentions another beast in verse

11: *"And I beheld another beast coming up out of the earth."* The Bible says that in the last days not only will there be the Antichrist to rule the world but another antichrist (the false prophet) to work with him.

"And he (the false prophet) doeth great wonders, so that he maketh fire come down from heaven on the earth in the sight of those miracles which he had power to do in the sight of the beast; saying to them that dwell on the earth, that they should make an image to the beast, which had the wound by a sword, and did live. And he had power to give life unto the image of the beast, that the image of the beast should both speak, and cause that as many as would not worship the image of the beast should be killed" (Revelation 13:13-15).

The demonically controlled false prophet will do miracles of a dimension to astound the skeptics. Finally the political and religious world will unite to destroy every true, Bible-believing Christian on earth at that time.

The Bible says, *"And he causeth all, both small and great, rich and poor, free and bond, to receive a mark in their right hand, or in their foreheads: and that no man might buy or sell, save he had the mark, or the name of the beast, or the number of his name. Here is wisdom. Let him that hath understanding count the number of the beast: for it is the number of a man; and his number is Six hundred threescore and six"* (Revelation 13:16-18). The world economy will be so organized that every buyer and seller will have a number by which to make transactions.

We are nearly to that point today! It is reported that there is a computer in Germany that has the capacity to keep track of every person on the face of the Earth. The beast, represented by a computer or not, will have absolute control. The mark of the beast will be stamped on the forehead or hand of every person who wants to survive. The mark will probably be invisible except when exposed to a certain light.

Whoever takes this mark of the beast will be sealed for the last-day judgments of God upon the earth. Revelation 19:20,21 records, *"...the beast was taken, and with him the false prophet that wrought miracles before him, with which he deceived them that had received the mark of the beast, and them that worshipped his image...And the remnant were slain with the sword of him that sat upon the horse, which sword proceeded out of his mouth: and all the fowls were filled with their flesh."* The beast and the false prophet, according to verse 20, *"were cast alive into a lake of fire burning with brimstone."*

The way events have been moving—with the world facing thermonuclear war, economic depression, with the call for a new government to preserve peace, with the coming of computers to keep track of every person on Earth, with the fulfillment of Bible prophecies—I believe the old scholar of Bible prophecy was right: "I think we are at the brink!"

John the apostle says, *"Little children, it is the last time: and as ye have heard that antichrist shall come, even now are there many antichrists; whereby we know that it is the last time. (...) But ye have an unction from the Holy One, and ye know all things" (1 John 2:18,20).* As a Christian, you have an anointing from the Holy Spirit that gives you guidance so you do not have to fear what is happening; you know what will take place, and you can have confidence in God. The Holy Spirit is our spiritual radar, who tells us when the storm is coming before it reaches us.

John says, *"Who is a liar but he that denieth*

the Father and the Son" (1 John 2:22). An individual who denies that Jesus Christ is the Son of God already has the spirit of Antichrist working in him. This fact should awaken many who know they should be saved, who know they should serve the Lord but who feel a spirit hindering them from making the right decision. The Antichrist will find its fulfillment in the beast and his doomed kingdom, but those who worship the Lord Jesus Christ will find everlasting life.

FIVE

The Scattered Sheep Come Home!

One of the greatest signs that we are living in the last days is the regathering of the Jewish people. The restoration of Israel fulfills many of the greatest prophecies in the Bible. Jesus often referred to the Jewish people as lost sheep. In Matthew 15:24, He said, *"...I am not sent but unto the lost sheep of the house of Israel."* In Matthew 10:6, He commanded His disciples to *"...go...to the lost sheep of the house of Israel."*

Consider the tremendous prophecy of Luke 21:24, *"...they (the Jews) shall fall by the edge of the sword, and shall be led away captive into all nations: and Jerusalem shall be trodden down of the Gentiles, until the times of the Gentiles be fulfilled."* Jesus said that when His scattered sheep returned to Israel and gained possession of Jerusalem, the "times of the Gentiles" would be at an end.

The phrase, "times of the Gentiles," is important: it refers first to the church age (God turned to the Gentiles to bring out a people for His name); and second, to the time when Gentile nations rule the world. At the end of the age, Jesus Christ will return to set up His Kingdom on Earth, and He will rule the world from the capital city, New Jerusalem. When the Jewish people return to Israel, when Jerusalem is no longer trodden down by the Gentiles, Gentile rule will end.

There is quite a story to the return of the scattered sheep. Nearly five hundred years before the birth of Christ, the Jewish people lost their political independence. At the time He was born, many Jews were looking for their promised Messiah. Daniel's prophecies told them when to expect Him *(cf. Daniel, chapter 9)*, but they did not expect the Messiah to come in the manner in which Jesus came.

They looked for a messiah who would drive the Romans from their land and liberate them

48

politically. Jesus Christ came to set them free spiritually. He knew that their greatest need was to be restored to a right relationship with God; He died to atone for the sins of the world and rose again in victory over death.

Jewish people have found the crucifixion difficult to understand in terms of their envisioned messiah, but Daniel foretold the Savior's death: *"...after threescore and two weeks shall Messiah be cut off, but not for himself..."* (Daniel 9:26a).

During His ministry, Jesus foretold Jerusalem's impending destruction: *"For the days shall come upon thee that thine enemies shall cast a trench about thee, and compass thee round, and keep thee in on every side, and shall lay thee even with the ground, and thy children within thee; and they shall not leave in thee one stone upon another; because thou knowest not the time of thy visitation"* (Luke 19:43,44). Forty years later the Roman general, Titus, and 80,000 Roman soldiers laid siege upon Jerusalem and the city fell.

The carnage was terrible. Josephus, a Jewish historian, recorded that more than one million Jews were slaughtered. More than one hundred thousand Jews were taken captive;

Egypt's slave markets were so glutted with Jewish slaves that a man sold for less than a horse. Titus carried away many of the Jewish nobles as slave trophies. The Arch of Triumph was erected in Rome to memorialize his victory.

All of this is a matter of recorded history, but remember that Jesus foretold these events 40 years before they happened. Because the first part of His prophecy came true, you can be assurred that the second part will be fulfilled.

Jesus said, *"...Jerusalem shall be trodden down of the Gentiles, until the times of the Gentiles be fulfilled" (Luke 21:24b)*! From A.D. 70, when Titus destroyed Jerusalem, until the beginning of the 1900s, very few Jews lived in the land then known as Palestine. The land lay desolate. In 1869, the American author, Mark Twain, penned, "Palestine sits in sackcloth and ashes. Over it broods the spell of a curse that has withered its fields and fettered its energies. Bethlehem and Bethany, in their poverty and in their humiliation, have nothing about them now to remind one that they once knew the high honor of the Savior's presence; the hallowed spot where the shepherds watched their flocks by night, where the angels sang, 'Peace on Earth, good will to men' is untenanted by any living creature and unblessed by any feature that is pleasant to the eye. Renewed Jerusalem itself, the stateliest name in history, has lost all its ancient grandeur and has become a pauper village.''

A miracle began to take place around 1900. The scattered sheep of the house of Israel began to return to their ancient homeland. The first return, or "aliyah," was in 1882. "Aliyah" means "the ascendancy" or "the going up." The second aliyah came after 1900; the third aliyah came after the British made the *Balfor Declaration* in 1917. The fourth return came in 1925. The fifth took place among the Jews who managed to escape Hitler's holocaust of World War II. The sixth aliyah happened when Israel was reborn in 1948. We are watching the continual return of the Jews to their homeland. Jesus said that when this happened the end of the age would be at hand.

Fifty thousand Jews living in Yemen felt the urge to return home in 1948. Their settlement was reported to be the oldest Jewish settlement in the world, yet the Yemenese Jews felt they must return to the land of their fathers.

Thousands of these Jews walked 300 miles across the desert and arrived at the airfield in Aden, a British protectorate on the southern tip of Arabia. Many of them were malnourished and sick with malaria.

The world didn't know what to do with them. When the United Nations decided to help them return home, the U.S. Air Force volunteered to fly them into Palestine. One of the Jews said, "For all these years we waited upon the Lord, and He kept renewing our strength; and now we're mounting up with the wings of eagles."

What kind of urgency would cause the oldest Jewish settlement in history to make an exodus to barren Palestine? Not long after this, communists took over Yemen; if the Jews had waited until then, they probably never would have made it to Palestine.

Scattered sheep from other countries began to cross the borders into Palestine. One hundred twenty-two thousand Jews returned to Palestine from Iraq. Eighty thousand Jews returned from Romania in 1951. Others came from Hungary and Czechoslovakia. The entire Jewish community of Yugoslavia returned to Palestine, and about forty-four thousand returned from Bulgaria. Between 1952 and 1956, thousands of Jews arrived from North Africa.

Since Israel became a nation, Jews from 100 nations have returned to their homeland. What does this mean? This is more than an ordinary population shift. This is a diving exodus, fulfilling the Bible prophecy that in the last days the scattered sheep would return to their homeland.

Hitler rose to power in the 1940s and turned upon the Jews with satanic fury. He incinerated at least six million souls, but his demonic deed turned world sympathy in favor of the Jews, with the result that the United Nations voted to make Palestine the Jewish homeland. Palestine was a desert, but there was plenty of room for the Jews and Arabs to live in peace.

Israel had become a state after 2500 years in exile! The scattered sheep began to return, and the Star of David flew over the nation. End-time prophecies of Ezekiel, Daniel and Jesus Christ were being fulfilled before the world's eyes.

Evangel Magazine reported that when the Jews ran their flag up in Jerusalem, the Jews went wild. Young and old—they climbed up on two-wheel oil carts used for gasoline and kerosene delivery and waved flags. An elderly Jewish man said, "I have been waiting since 1885 for this great event, and it is time for the Messiah to come! It's time for the Messiah to come!"

The Arabs attacked, attempting to wipe the small nation out, but the Israelis couldn't be beaten. Lewis Hauff, in his book, *Israel in Bible Prophecy*, wrote, "A pastor in Jerusalem told us the victory of Israel against overwhelming odds was a miracle. Six hundred fifty thousand Jews were surrounded by 40 million Arabs, with one and one-half million of them armed. Eighty thousand Jews in Jerusalem were cut off from the rest of the people of Israel. Only a miracle could save them."

The military miracle happened, and Israel was saved. The Israelis not only won the war in 1948 but the war in 1956 and again in June 1967. During the 1967 war the Jews regained possession of the old city of Jerusalem and the Wailing Wall, fulfilling Jesus' prophecy in Luke 21:24, *"...Jerusalem shall be trodden down of the Gentiles, until the times of the Gentiles be fulfilled."*

The church age is coming to a close.

The time of Gentile world dominion is soon to cease.

Now is the time for the Messiah to come. The scattered sheep of the house of Israel are returning. They have come close to the fold, and the Shepherd must be nearby.

SIX

The Coming Kingdom of the Lamb!

Despite fearful events taking place throughout the world today, the Bible assures us that this planet has a grand and glorious future. In Revelation, chapters 20 and 21, you can read about the wonderful events to take place when Jesus Christ, the Lamb of God, sets up His Kingdom upon earth.

For centuries Christians have prayed, "Thy kingdom come, thy will be done." God will answer these prayers by revealing the coming Kingdom of the Lamb in power.

The future is filled with great events: first the return of Jesus Christ for His church; second, the Russian armies will invade Israel and be defeated through Divine intervention; third, the Antichrist will rise to power; fourth, a time of terrifying Tribulation will seize the world; fifth, the visible return of Jesus Christ to Earth. The Lamb will set up His Kingdom and reign forever and ever.

The Bible tells us what will happen when Christ returns at the end of the Tribulation period: *"And I saw an angel come down from heaven, having the key of the bottomless pit and a great chain in his hand. And he laid hold on the dragon, that old serpent, which is the Devil, and Satan, and bound him a thousand years, and cast him into the bottomless pit, and shut him up, and set a seal upon him, that he should deceive the nations no more, till the thousand years should be fulfilled..."* (Revelation 20:1-3b).

For centuries Satan has run back and forth throughout the Earth as a roaring lion. During the first one thousand years of Christ's reign, Satan will be locked in the bottomless pit—this accuser of the brethren, this prince of liars will be bound in chains. Satan will then be loosed for a short time, and then he will be cast into the lake of fire; he will never be allowed to tempt men again.

The second step in the coming Kingdom of the Lamb will be the establishment of a new world government. The Bible says, *"And I saw the thrones, and they that sat upon them, and judgment was given unto them: and I saw the souls of them that were beheaded for the witness of Jesus, and for the Word of God, and which had not worshipped the beast, neither his image, neither had received his mark upon their foreheads, or in their hands; and they lived and reigned with Christ a thousand years"* (Revelation 20:4).

The saints of God will be given leadership positions in the Kingdom of the Lamb—they will rule the world. Unbelievers are in power today, but when Jesus Christ returns He will reward His faithful followers. The Bible says, *"If we suffer, we shall also reign with him..."* (2 Timothy 2:12a).

The third step in the coming Kingdom of the Lamb will be the Great White Throne Judgment! Matthew 25:31 and Revelation 20:11 foretell this awesome courtroom event. John says, *"...I saw a great white throne, and him that sat on it, from whose face the earth and the heaven fled away; and there was found no place for them. And I saw the dead, small and great, stand before God; and the books were opened: and another book was opened, which is the book of life: and the dead were judged out of those things which were written in the books, according to their works. And the sea gave up the dead which were in it; and death and hell delivered up the dead which were in them: and they were judged every man according to their works. And death and hell were cast into the lake of fire. This is the second death. And whosoever was not found written in the book of life was cast into the lake of fire" (Revelation 20:11-15).* God will judge the world at the very beginning of the Kingdom of the Lamb.

The fourth step in the coming Kingdom of the Lamb will be the creation of a new heaven! Today the heavens are magnificent, but in the future they will be even more wonderful. God will cleanse them of all the burned-out satellites, abandoned spacecraft and radioactive debris that will have cluttered them after the terrible Tribulation.

We do not have a description of what the new heavens will be like, but we can imagine that the darkness of outer space will be lifted and we will see an even greater masterpiece to the glory of the Creator.

The fifth step in the coming Kingdom of the Lamb will be the creation of a new Earth. The Bible says, *"...I saw a new heaven and a new earth: for the first heaven and the first earth were passed away; and there was no more sea" (Revelation 21:1)*. Pollution, atomic radiation, erosion and a host of other abuses have made Earth almost uninhabitable in many places, but God will cleanse the Earth with fire.

The apostle Peter prophesied, *"...the day of the Lord will come as a thief in the night; in which the heavens shall pass away with a great noise, and the elements shall melt with fervent heat, the earth also and the works therein shall be burned up" (2 Peter 3:10)*. God will then remodel Earth into the paradise it was before man corrupted it; everything will be perfect and beautiful beyond description.

The sixth step in the coming Kingdom of the Lamb will be the removal of the sea! John says in Revelation 21:1, *"...there was no more sea."* Two thirds of the globe are covered by water but one day the seas will be gone. Some Bible scholars think God will divide the waters as in Genesis, so the waters will be above the

Earth, forming a greenhouse effect so the world will be shielded from the sun's harmful radiation.

The seventh step in the future Kingdom of the Lamb will be a new capital city! The Bible says, *"...I John saw the holy city, new Jerusalem, coming down from God out of heaven, prepared as a bride adorned for her husband. And I heard a great voice out of heaven saying, Behold, the tabernacle of God is with men, and he will dwell with them, and they shall be his people, and God himself shall be with them, and be their God"* (Revelation 21:2,3).

An angel showed John *"...that great city, the holy Jerusalem, descending out of heaven from God, having the glory of God: and her light was like unto a stone most precious, even like a jasper stone, clear as crystal; and had a wall great and high, and had twelve gates, and at the gates twelve angels, and names written thereon, which are the names of the twelve tribes of the children of Israel.*

"(...) And the twelve gates were twelve pearls; every several gate was of one pearl: and the street of the city was pure gold, as it were transparent glass. And I saw no temple

therein: for the Lord God Almighty and the Lamb are the temple of it. And the city had no need of the sun, neither of the moon, to shine in it: for the glory of God did lighten it, and the Lamb is the light thereof" (Revelation 21:10b-12,21-23).

The description in the Book of Revelation is far more complete, but we can see from the above excerpt that the Holy City will be beautiful beyond imagination. Jesus said to His followers, *"...I go to prepare a place for you" (cf. John 14:2).* When God created the world, as described in Genesis, chapter 1, he turned a formless planet within a void into a perfect dwelling for humanity within six days. Can you imagine the stunning perfection of the Holy City? God has been working on it for nearly two thousand years! No wonder the Bible says, *"...Eye hath not seen, nor ear heard, neither have entered into the heart of man, the things which God hath prepared for them that love him" (1 Corinthians 2:9).*

This beautiful city will be our home for eternity; every saint will have a place in this city. Seiss points out in his commentary on the Apocalypse, "...the length and breadth and the height of (the New Jerusalem) are equal.

Here would be streets over streets, and stories over stories—up, up, up, to the height of 1500 miles—and each street is 1500 miles long. Thus this city is a solid cube of golden construction 1500 miles every way." The base would stretch from farthest Maine to farthest Florida, and from the shore of the Atlantic to Colorado. The magnitude of this new capital city is so astonishing it is hard to believe. Remember, if you belong to Christ this city is the place that Jesus Christ has prepared for you. This will be your glorious home for all eternity.

The Bible says this Holy City will be supernaturally illuminated: "...the city had no need of the sun, neither of the moon, to shine in it: for the glory of God did lighten it, and the Lamb is the light thereof" (Revelation 21:23). There won't be any electrical wiring or transformers to clutter up the Holy City; the light of God will radiate from every stone! One of the most thrilling discoveries by astronomers in recent times has been the great empty space in the nebula of the Orion constellation: a heavenly cavern so gigantic that the mind of man cannot comprehend it and so brilliantly beautiful that words cannot adequately describe it. Powerful telescopes, utilizing long-exposure photographic plates, can peer into the depths of interstellar space and glimpse its vastness.

The opening within the Orion constellation is perhaps more than 16 trillion, 740 billion miles in diameter. The diameter of the Earth's orbit is 186 million miles, but the Orion opening is 90 thousand times as wide! Thirty thousand solar systems like ours could be stretched side-by-side across the entrance of the Orion opening and there would be room to spare. Surpassing the immensity of its size is its exquisite beauty. The luminous colors are unlike any upon Earth.

Professor Learkin of Mount Lowe Observatory gives us the following description of the Orion nebula: "These photographs reveal the opening and interior of a cavern so stupendous that our entire solar system would be lost therein. I have watched it since the days of youth in many telescopes of many powers, but never dreamed that the central region is the mouth of a colossal cave. Pen of writer and brush of artist alike are lifeless and inert in any attempt to describe this interior.

"For the depths of the Orion nebula appear like torn and twisted objects and river masses of shining glass, irregular pillars, columns of stalactites in glittering splendor and stalagmites from the mighty floor. The appearance is like that of light shining and glowing behind the clear walls of ivory and pearl, studded with millions of diamond shining stars."

There must be a reason for all this grandeur. Could this be heaven itself? If heaven is this spectacular, imagine what the Holy City will be like! God is planning spectacular things for His redeemed people.

SEVEN

They'll Blame It on the UFOs!

Surprisingly, many Christians are unaware that Jesus Christ is going to return—suddenly, without warning—to catch His church away before the great Tribulation judgments of God fall upon the Earth.

Jesus Christ gave us His guarantee that He will return: *"Let not your heart be troubled; ye believe in God, believe also in me. In my Father's house are many mansions: if it were not so, I would have told you. I go to prepare a place for you. And if I go and prepare a place for you, I will come again, and receive you unto myself; that where I am, there ye may be also"* (John 14:1-3).

The day Jesus ascended into heaven, two

angels appeared and said, *"...Ye men of Galilee, why stand ye gazing into heaven? this same Jesus, which is taken up from you into heaven, shall so come in like manner as ye have seen him go into heaven" (Acts 1:11).*

The apostle Paul reminded the Christians at Corinth that every time they received communion they should consider Christ's return: *"For as often as ye eat this bread, and drink this cup, ye do shew the Lord's death till he come" (1 Corinthians 11:26).*

In 1 Thessalonians 4:16 Paul said, *"For the Lord himself shall descend from heaven with a shout, with the voice of the archangel, and with the trump of God: and the dead in Christ shall rise first: Then we which are alive and remain shall be caught up together with them in the clouds, to meet the Lord in the air: and so shall we ever be with the Lord."*

Just imagine for a moment. You are a born-again Christian; you have heard and read about the soon return of Jesus Christ; and you have been looking for His appearing. This day you feel an unusual feeling of expectancy, a remarkable awareness of the Lord's presence, and you go about your regular activities with praise in your heart!

Suddenly it happens. You feel a sudden lift (much like the feeling you receive when a rapidly rising elevator stops), only *this time you keep going!* You're free! Your body has changed in an instant, and you begin to rise in much the same manner as those who have described out-of-the-body, life-after-life experiences. You see Earth disappearing in the distance.

Soon you begin to notice others rising with you. A sweet calm wells within your soul, and you are comforted with a sense of well-being. It's like you are floating upward at a remarkable speed. You can hear singing and rejoicing; others around you are praising God.

Everything happened so suddenly that you didn't have time to figure it out until now— Jesus Christ returned, and you are being caught up to be with Him!

Earth is in pandemonium. Millions are missing. Airplanes have crashed because Christian pilots have been snatched from their cockpits. Buses and automobiles have careened wildly into other lanes of traffic. There is death and confusion. Unbelieving parents discover their Christian children are missing. Husbands go berserk when they realize their Christian wives have been taken.

TV and radio networks go on emergency alert. The National Guard is called out. The cities of the world are in bedlam; people are running madly in the streets, screaming the names of their departed loved ones.

To the unbelieving world—which denied that Jesus Christ was God's Son—the return **of Jesus Christ for His church will sound far-**fetched. People will try to find some other explanation for the global catastrophe.

I have a feeling they will blame it on the UFOs. Now, I really haven't come to a conclusion as to what the UFOs really are. All I know is that too many honest people have testified about some UFOs to discount their stories. Until the facts are known, whenever someone asks me about the UFOs I will continue to reply, "They are unidentified flying objects!"

Newspapers, magazines, TV programs and motion pictures have been filled with stories about unusual spacecraft; and I think when millions of Christians are caught away to be with Jesus Christ, many will blame UFOs for their disappearance.

I personally believe Christ's return will take

place before the great Tribulation described by the prophets Isaiah and Daniel and others, as well as by our Lord Himself and the apostle John in the Book of Revelation. The reason I believe He will return before the Tribulation— particularly the last three and one-half years when God's wrath is poured out upon the Earth—is as follows.

Jesus continually warned believers to be prepared so they would escape the judgments of God. In Luke 21:34-36 He said, "...*take heed to yourselves, lest at any time your hearts be overcharged with surfeiting, and drunkenness, and cares of this life, and so that day come upon you unawares. For as a snare shall it come on all them that dwell on the face of the whole earth. Watch ye therefore, and pray always, that ye may be accounted worthy to escape all these things that shall come to pass, and to stand before the Son of man.*"

In Matthew 24:44 Jesus said, "*Therefore be ye also ready: for in such an hour as ye think not the Son of man cometh.*" In Matthew 25:13 He said, "*Watch therefore, for ye know neither the day nor the hour wherein the Son of man cometh.*"

I do not believe the church will go through

the Tribulation period; the last three and one-half years of that seven-year period is God's time of judgment upon the unbelieving world. God certainly will not punish His chosen children with the unbelievers—no more than a general would command troops to fire upon a village that housed his wife and children.

Remember, God rescued Noah by means of the ark before He sent the flood *(cf. Genesis 6:18)*.

Remember, God rescued Lot by the angels before He rained fire upon Sodom and Gomorrah *(cf. Genesis 19:12-15)*.

Remember, Jesus Christ warned believers to flee Jerusalem before the Romans attacked the city in A.D. 70: *"...when ye shall see Jerusalem compassed with armies, then know that the desolation thereof is nigh. Then let them which are in Judea flee to the mountains: and let them which are in the midst of it depart out; and let not them that are in the countries enter thereinto. But woe to them that are with child, and to them that give suck, in those days! for there shall be great distress in the land, and wrath upon these people"* (Luke 21:20-23). History confirms that when the Roman armies surrounded Jerusalem the Christians remembered these words of Christ and fled the city.

There will be a more complete fulfillment of this prophecy and escape during the time of tribulation, but Jesus did tell His people to flee so they would not receive the wrath upon the city.

The Bible clearly teaches that the heart of God is tender toward his children. His chosen **church will not suffer the judgment poured out upon unbelievers.**

The apostle Paul wrote to the Christians in Thessalonica, *"For God hath not appointed us to wrath, but to obtain salvation by our Lord Jesus Christ"* (1 Thessalonians 5:9). Paul wrote to the Christians at Corinth, *"Behold, I shew you a mystery; we shall not all sleep, but we shall all be changed, in a moment, in the twinkling of an eye, at the last trump: for the trumpet shall sound, and the dead shall be raised incorruptible, and we shall be changed"* (1 Corinthians 15:51,52).

Many unbelievers will probably blame the disappearance of Christian people on the UFOs; but as for those in the know, they will be on the go, rejoicing with the Lord and all of their loved ones who have gathered in heaven. To some, the soon return of Jesus Christ and the catching-away of His church sound like science fiction; and yet those who know their Bibles and love the Lord will experience the catching-away of His church as spiritual fact.

Here is what the apostle Paul declared: *"...there shall come in the last days scoffers, walking after their own lusts, and saying, Where is the promise of his coming? for since the fathers fell asleep, all things continue as they were from the beginning of creation. For this they are willingly ignorant of..."* (2 Peter 3:3-5a).

Years ago Hank Williams wrote in a song, "I'll never get out of this world alive." He should have read the Bible and learned of the one great, glorious exception. Christians, who are living at the time of our Lord's return, are going to get out of this world alive. They won't be on board some unidentified flying object. They will be with Jesus Christ, the identified Son of the Living God, who conquered death, who arose from the grave and ascended to the Father's right hand in glory.

Jesus Christ is coming soon for those who look for His appearing!

EIGHT

The Unexpected Judgment!

Many Christians are going to be in for a surprise when Jesus Christ returns: there will be a judgment!

The apostle Paul told the Philippian Christians, *"For I am in a strait betwixt two, having a desire to depart, and to be with Christ; which is far better: nevertheless to abide in the flesh is more needful for you"* (Philippians 1:23,24). He knew that going to heaven would be a great experience but that God wanted him—and the Philippian Christians—to minister in the world.

As Christians, we are the "salt of the earth" *(cf. Matthew 5:13)* and we will face a special judgment before Almighty God after Jesus

Christ returns for us. Paul wrote to the Christians in Rome, *"...we shall all stand before the judgment seat of Christ. ...So then every one of us shall give account of himself to God"* (Romans 14:10,12).

Most Christians realize there will be a great White Throne Judgment at the end of the world when God judges the wicked dead, but they have overlooked the judgment of the righteous! This unexpected judgment will reveal the quality of works performed by Christian people, and it will determine their rewards. As far as some Christians are concerned, they will appear bankrupt when they face God.

The Bible says, *"For other foundation can no man lay than that is laid, which is Jesus Christ. Now if any man build upon this foundation gold, silver, precious stones, wood, hay, stubble; every man's work shall be made manifest: for the day shall declare it, because it shall be revealed by fire; and the fire shall try every man's work of what sort it is. If any man's work abide which he hath built thereupon, he shall receive a reward. If any man's work shall be burned, he shall suffer loss: but he himself shall be saved: yet so as by fire"* (1

Corinthians 3:11-15).

Fire will try the works of Christian people at the Judgment Seat of Christ. I believe I know where that fire comes from. In Revelation, John saw Jesus Christ and said, *"His head and hairs were white like wool, as white as snow; and his eyes were as a flame of fire; and his feet like unto fine brass, as if they burned in a furnace; and his voice as the sound of many waters. And he had in his right hand seven stars: and out of his mouth went a sharp two-edged sword: and his countenance was as the sun shineth in his strength"* (Revelation 1:14-16). When Jesus Christ, in His great glory, looks at our works with His eyes aflame with fire, I believe that every work that has been done without the purest motive will be burned in a moment.

We can see from the teachings of the Bible that not every Christian will have the same reward in heaven. Some will be greatly blessed, and others will be *"saved; yet so as by fire."*

In Luke, Jesus told His apostles, *"Ye are they which have continued with me in my temptations. And I appoint unto you a kingdom, as my Father hath appointed unto me; that ye may eat and drink at my table in my* kingdom, and sit on thrones judging the twelve tribes of Israel" (Luke 22:28-30). The 12 apostles will rule over the 12 tribes of Israel, but other Christians will be saved by the skin of their teeth.

The teaching of the Judgment Seat of Christ was never meant to imply that a man can save himself from the punishment of sin through good works, for the Bible clearly states, "For by grace are ye saved through faith; and that not of yourselves: it is the gift of God: not of works, lest any man should boast" (Ephesians 2:8,9).

Even though we will not be saved by works, we will be rewarded according to our works. Works are very important. Our faithfulness to Jesus Christ in giving Him our best service will make a tremendous difference on the day when the rewards are given out!

This is crucial teaching for every Christian, because I sense in some of God's people a re-laxed, "I'm saved now, I have nothing to worry about" attitude. After coming to Christ we shouldn't relax and take it easy. This would be as inconsiderate as someone saved from drowning to calmly walk up the beach as hundreds of other drowning souls cry out from the water. We are saved by grace, but our works determine our rewards.

It's like a man who is too poor to buy a wheelbarrow and a concerned neighbor gives him one. Now the fellow has a wheelbarrow, but what he puts into the wheelbarrow after it's given to him determines how far ahead he will get in life. God by His grace gives us salvation, but He expects us to be faithful servants of the Living Christ.

The question facing you as a Christian is whether or not you are prepared for this "Unexpected Judgment Seat of Christ." If Jesus Christ returned today and you were to stand before Him, could you say that you had given Him your very best effort? In that day some unfaithful Christian will say, "Lord, I never realized how important it was for me to give you my best. I always thought I was saved by grace and that was all I needed—but now I see that I should have given you my best effort in service." Another might say, "Lord, let me live my Christian life one more time. Why, if you will just give me another chance, I will pray more, Lord. I will read my Bible more. I will witness more. I could help my pastor build the church. I could support ministries everywhere. Lord, please give me another chance!"

But there will not be a second chance.

You are living now—in the last days. If you would make any change in your life, you had better make it now. The return of Jesus Christ is at hand.

The Bible says, *"When Christ, who is our life, shall appear, then shall we also appear with him in glory. Mortify* (or put to death) *therefore your members which are upon the earth: fornication* (that is sex before marriage), *inordinate affection, evil concupiscence* (that is unbridled sexual desire), *and covetousness, which is idolatry: for which things' sake the wrath of God cometh on the children of disobedience: in the which ye also walked sometime, when ye lived in them. But now ye also put off all these; anger, wrath, malice, blasphemy, filthy communication out of your mouth. Lie not one to another, seeing that ye have put off the old man with his deeds; and have put on the new man, which is renewed in knowledge after the image of him that created him..." (Colossians 3:4-10).*

Jesus Christ is coming soon, and you need to make every effort to live a holy life and extend His Gospel.

The Lord who loved you and died for your sins is asking you for your commitment. Will you give Him your very best? It's one thing to go to church and sit on the bench and live an easy life, just to hum along with the songs and go along with the message without ever really committing your inner self to them. It's another thing to say, "Lord, my body is a temple of yours. I give it to you as a living sacrifice. Take me, Lord. I want to be of service to you so that when you return you will be able to look at me and say, 'Well done, thou good and faithful servant.'"

NINE

The Last Great Judgment!

The most awesome day in the history of eternity will be the last great Judgment. Judgment Day is plainly taught by the prophets and is rooted in the conscience of man. Daniel declared, *"...many of them that sleep in the dust of the earth shall awake, some to everlasting life, and some to shame and everlasting contempt"* (Daniel 12:2).

The apostle John had a vision of the last great Judgment and said, *"...I saw a great white throne, and him that sat on it, from whose face the earth and the heaven fled away; and there was found no place for them. And I saw the dead, small and great, stand before God; and the books were opened: and another book was opened, which is the book of life: and the dead were judged out of those things which were written in the books, according to their works. And the sea gave up the dead which were in it; and death and hell delivered up the dead which were in them; and they were judged every man according to their works. And death and hell were cast into the lake of fire. This is the second death. And whosoever was not found written in the book of life was cast into the lake of fire" (Revelation 20:11-15).*

This prophecy is one of the most important portions in Holy Scripture: it tells you how to prepare for the Last Judgment.

Christians will appear at the Judgment Seat of Christ to account for their Christian service, but this last great Judgment is reserved for the wicked dead of all the ages. As Daniel said, *"...many of them that sleep in the dust of the earth shall awake, some to everlasting life, and some to shame and everlasting contempt."*

Some people will be saved and others lost. The saved that appear at that moment must be those who served God the best they knew how prior to the coming of Christ, for the Bible clearly teaches that His saints will be judged at the Judgment Seat of Christ. John said, *"...I saw the dead, small and great, stand before God; and the books were opened: and another book was opened, which is the book of life: and the dead were judged out of those things which were written in the books, according to their works"* (Revelation 20:12). Renowned caesars, kings and queens, pharaohs, and others including Hitler and Stalin will appear with millions of "unknowns" before God.

I believe the saints of the ages will be there too, not as defendants but as witnesses. Perhaps when the wicked dead are judged and found guilty, many will cry out, "Why isn't so-and-so here? Why isn't my brother here? Why isn't my friend here?" God will ask those persons who had repented and received Christ to step forward, and they will testify before the condemned as to why they were saved.

All of humanity will be assembled at the Last Judgment. John declared, *"...I saw the dead, small and great, stand before God; and the books were opened..."* (Revelation 20:12a). God has kept a personal record for every single person, from the date of birth to death. Modern computers can keep a detailed account of an individual's lifetime of financial dealings and recall it all within a moment. God has kept a detailed account, not only of our deeds but of our thoughts, wishes and secret plans. At the last great Judgment, Jesus said: *"...there is nothing covered, that shall not be revealed; neither hid, that shall not be known. Therefore whatsoever ye have spoken in darkness shall be heard in the light; and that which ye have spoken in the ear in closets shall be proclaimed upon the house tops"* (Luke 12:2,3). There really aren't any secrets; the books at the Judgment will reveal everything.

"...Another book was opened, which is the book of life..." (Revelation 20:12). The existence of this book will come as a surprise to many people who instinctively realize they will have to give account for their actions at Judgment Day. There are going to be two books. The second book is called *The Lamb's Book of Life.* In this book are the names of all the men and women and children who have received Jesus Christ as their personal Savior. The moment you repent, the moment you are born again, your name goes into the *Lamb's Book* of the redeemed.

The Bible says, *"...and the dead were*

judged out of those things which were written in the books, according to their works" (Revelation 20). No one will escape the facts that follow them to the Judgment.

"And the sea gave up the dead which were in it..." (Revelation 20:13). Even the unbelievers who have had their bodies cremated and their ashes strewn to the winds in order to annihilate any form of their existence will appear with all of mankind at the Last Judgment *(cf. 2 Corinthians 5:10).*

"...They were judged every man according to their works" (Revelation 20:13). Again, and again, and again, John is gripped by the systematic, unrelenting judgment of the wicked dead!

"And death and hell were cast into the lake of fire. This is the second death" (Revelation 20:14). John declared that a man can die twice. He dies once when his body is cast into the ground. He dies again when God casts his soul into the lake of fire. If a man is only born once, he dies twice. But if he is born twice, he only dies once. If this sounds like a mystery, think about these words: if you are born physically and not born again spiritually, you will die twice; you will die when your body is

placed in the grave and again when your entire person (body, soul and spirit) is cast into the lake of fire.

If you are born twice, physically and then spiritually into God's family, you will only die once. You will die when your body is placed in the ground, but you will never have to fear the second death at the Last Judgment!

John's final statement in the passage is this: *"...whosoever was not found written in the book of life was cast into the lake of fire" (Revelation 20:15)*. Millions of so-called good people—who have had what appeared to be morally upright lives, who have had no time for Jesus Christ—will be shocked beyond words when they discover that God is going to pronounce "Guilty" upon everyone whose name is not written in the *Lamb's Book of Life*.

This always brings up the question, "What about the heathen who never heard of Jesus Christ?" I believe the Bible is correct where it says, *"Shall not the Judge of all the earth do right?" (Genesis 18:25c)*. I know God will be fair with those who have never heard the Gospel. I cannot say what their judgment will be, but I do know that Jesus said the heathen will be beaten with fewer stripes *(cf. Luke 12:48a)*. He was alluding to mercy of some dimension, but He did not describe the matter further. I think Jesus would not say more because lazy Christians would stay home in their easy chairs instead of spreading the Gospel and watch the world go to hell.

You and I cannot claim the ignorance of the heathen. You and I have heard the Gospel. We know that God loved us, that Jesus Christ died for our sins, and the reason He died for us was because we could not save ourselves.

Some time ago I was seated next to a Memphis businessman on a flight to Philadelphia. When I began to share the good news of Jesus Christ with him, he was insulted and retorted, "Mr. Lundstrom, I want you to know that I am a good man.!" What could I say? Then the Spirit of God gave me the answer. "Sir," I replied, "you are a good man, but you are not good enough." After we reviewed the Ten Commandments, he admitted that he had broken many of them, just as all of us have. Then I said, "The reason Jesus Christ died for you was that, though you were a good man, you weren't good enough!"

If there is so much as one sin on a person's

record, that person will not be saved unless he or she receives Jesus Christ as Savior. God is perfect and holy, and He demands holiness and perfection. This is why the *Lamb's Book of Life* is critical to your salvation! God knew we would sin, and He provided a Savior for us. Jesus Christ suffered our death when He died on the cross. If you will receive Him as your personal Savior, God will forgive you and write your name in the *Lamb's Book of Life*.

The story is told of an old Methodist minister who dreamed that he died and went to heaven. When he arrived at heaven's gate, the angels told him he couldn't be admitted.

The minister was shocked and said, "There must be some mistake! Go in and tell God I'm out here."

The angel went in and returned with the same message. God would not allow him to enter heaven.

Then the minister began to plead. He told the angels of the many years he had preached, how he had sacrificed to carry the Gospel to the little churches on his circuit, how he had ridden his horse through the rain and the snow and the cold, and of the many other sacrifices he had made for Jesus Christ.

The angel was so moved by the minister's story that he went back to the throne, and a few minutes later he reappeared and said, "God has granted you permission to plead your own case before His throne."

The gates of heaven swung open, and the minister was ushered into the Lord's presence. Everything was so holy and pure that the minister began to feel unworthy. When he reached the steps to the throne he did not dare to lift his eyes to behold God.

As he stood there with head bowed, overwhelmed by the holiness and majesty of Almighty God, he began to weep. He realized at that moment that he would never be good enough. He could never be religious enough. He would never be able to pray enough prayers to make it into heaven.

Then he felt the presence of Jesus Christ. Jesus came up and stood by his side and slipped His arm around the minister's waist; He looked up to the Father and said, "This is one of mine."

God replied, "It is well!"

The minister awakened from his dream, but he was never the same man again. He knew the only reason he would ever get to heaven was that he belonged to Jesus Christ.

That is our only reason.

Life in Eternity!

Part 1

Have you ever wondered what eternal life will be like?

To many, eternal life sounds boring. They imagine they will be sitting on a wet cloud, floating around heaven, playing a harp while ghost-like angels sing hymns. Some people think eternity in heaven will mean attending one endless church service.

The truth is that eternal life with God will be the most exciting experience imaginable!

The Bible says, *"...Eye hath not seen, nor ear heard, neither have entered into the heart of man, the things which God hath prepared for them that love him. But God hath revealed them unto us by his Spirit: for the Spirit* searcheth all things, yea, the deep things of God" (1 Corinthians 2:9,10). No one can ever fathom what heaven is like until the Spirit of God reveals its glory to him.

The apostle Paul said, "...now we see through a glass, darkly; but then face to face: now I know in part: but then shall I know even as also I am known" (1 Corinthians 13:12). Looking at life in eternity is like peering through dark glass; but even then, if you will look long and hard enough, you will see sights unspeakable and full of glory.

Critics often say no one could know about heaven because no one has ever been there. That is not true. Jesus Christ came from heaven, and He has described much of life after death for us. Just before He went to the garden of Gethsemane, He prayed a prayer to the Father in heaven that reveals something about eternal life that many have missed: "...O Father, glorify thou me with thine own self with the glory which I had with thee before the world was" (John 17:5). Jesus was soon to take back the powers and position He had voluntarily relinquished when He came into the world as a baby in Bethlehem. He would soon be liberated from His earthly body of flesh and blood. He would be free from the pull of gravity in Earth's atmosphere. He would be free from pain and suffering, free from death, free from the burden of the world's sin. He would be free from the passage of time and limited space.

This is the glory that men and women are yearning for today although they do not realize it. Have you noticed how many TV programs and motion pictures express this cosmic longing? *Star Wars, Star-Trek, Superman, The Six-Million-Dollar Man, Wonder Woman* and *Battlestar Galactica* are just a few. As Bill Popejoy has said, "God helps us become aware of the brevity of time and the endlessness of eternity. He teaches us a truth that we innately knew but didn't know how to put into words—that we were made for another world."

The Bible teaches us many truths about eternal life.

First, we will have new, supernatural bodies! After His resurrection, Jesus Christ had a new, supernatural body. He was able to leave His grave bindings behind without disturbing their arrangement. He could pass through doors without opening them.

Do you remember how the disciples feared for their lives after the crucifixion of Jesus Christ? They huddled together in a room, wondering when they would be captured and nailed to crosses for following Him. Suddenly He materialized before their eyes! Jesus said to Thomas, *"...Reach hither thy finger, and behold my hands: and reach hither thy hand, and thrust it into my side: and be not faithless, but believing. And Thomas answered and said unto him, My Lord and my God"* (John 20:27,28).

Jesus Christ was able to move in both the spirit and material world. Einstein said if any material substance could reach the speed of light it would be able to pass through another substance without disturbing the molecular structure. In other words, if you could throw a baseball at the speed of light, it could pass through a brick wall without disturbing either the brick or the ball! Einstein also said, "If you travel at the speed of light, space shrinks to zero, time increases to infinity."

Jesus said, *"...I am the light of the world"* (John 8:12). He, the Creator of the universe, is able to move at the speed of light! The Lord's spiritual body is not restricted by time, space or mass; and your spiritual body in the resurrection, if you are a Christian, will be like His.

In his letter to the Philippian Christians, Paul says that Jesus *"...shall change our vile body, that it may be fashioned like unto his glorious body, according to the working whereby he is able even to subdue all things unto himself"* (Philippians 3:21).

Your spiritual body will be free from pain and death, and because eternity is timeless you will never age. Your spiritual body will be incorruptible, glorious, powerful. As the caterpillar emerges from the chrysalis a beautiful butterfly, free from the limitations of a worm, you will break away from the bondage of your earthly body: *"...as we have borne the image of the earthy, we shall also bear the image of the heavenly"* (1 Corinthians 15:49).

Often when the subject of a new spiritual body comes up in a discussion, someone will ask, "Why doesn't God allow sexual reproduction in eternity?" Jesus said, *"...in the resurrection they neither marry, nor are given in marriage, but are as the angels of God in heaven"* (Matthew 22:30). Many who enjoy the pleasures of flesh in this life would think this world offers more pleasure than life in eternity. C. S. Lewis humorously describes the situation with the story of a father who was trying to explain the pleasure of sexual intimacy to his little boy.

The father said, "Son, when you grow older you will most likely find a girl you love, and you will want to be with her always. You will desire to know her in a physically intimate way."

The boy, who did not understand sexual desires, replied, "Dad, can I eat chocolates at the same time?"

When some people think of life in eternity, they are so physically minded they cannot imagine spiritual pleasures beyond the physical delights they have known.

Second, your life in eternity will be free of time! There won't be sundials, watches or calendars. You will live in the everlasting present! The Bible says, *"...that there should be time no longer" (Revelation 10:6).*

Can you imagine the effects of timelessness? There will be no "then" because we will live in the eternal "now," no "there" because all will be "here" in a universe filled with the glory of God.

I have met many people who could have become great singers, artists, architects, teachers and leaders if only they had the time and opportunity to develop their talents. Praise God! Christian people who struggled through existence on Earth will have the privilege of developing their abilities throughout eternity!

Architects will build cities, singers will perform in concerts and actors will perform in plays. Musical composers will become so masterful that their works will make the compositions of Mozart and Handel sound childish.

You will have all of the time and resources you need to do everything you could wish to come true.

Third, your eternal life will be one of service. Revelation 22:3 says, *"...there shall be no more curse: but the throne of God and of the Lamb shall be in it; and his servants shall serve him."*

Eternity will be filled with activity. Service—I love the thought of it! The happiest people in the world are the busiest people. Revelation 7:15 says, *"...they (are) before the throne of God, and serve him day and night in his temple: and he that sitteth on the throne shall dwell among them.''*

Can you imagine the excitement of serving God—having God's wisdom, God's power, God's resources and God's timelessness to complete your task?

Eternal life with God is the ultimate experience known to mortal man. Only when we are with Him will we realize what He has meant us to be. We shall share His glory, the glory of His only begotten Son, our Lord Jesus Christ, forever.

ELEVEN

Life in Eternity!

Is there hope?

The story is told that Winston Churchill asked the famous young evangelist, Billy Graham, "Is there hope for the world?"

I wonder what Churchill would say today.

The nations of the world are spending more than $1 billion a day on armaments.

Russia has risen to become the number-one military power on the globe.

Red China will be able to buy the technology she needs to become a military menace since the United States has granted her diplomatic recognition.

Since the Shah of Iran has been thrown out, the oil flowing to the U.S. is uncertain and the price is rising. Some predict that gasoline will rise to $1.25 per gallon.

Since Europe is on-the-grow and Christians who are in-the-know realize that the Antichrist is coming to power and he will cause the world to tremble...

Is there hope?

Billy Graham gave Winston Churchill the answer that still holds true. He said, "I *know* there is hope because I have read the last chapter of the Bible!"

In Revelation, the last book in the Bible, God gave the apostle John a vision of the future. In this revelation John heard the Lord say, "*...Behold, I make all things new*" *(Revelation 21:5).* This is the hope that overcomes the fearful things taking place in our world today. God is going to make all things new. He is going to make new heavens and a new Earth. God is going to establish a new government. Eternity will be a panorama of His power and majesty. If we can see the future as bright as it really is, we will be buoyed up no matter what happens until then.

When I was a small boy, my father would often take me to the large pasture in the hills where he kept his cattle for the summer season; it was an expanse of several hundred acres that he rented from the Indians. Dad would count his cattle every week because he left them unattended and he wanted to be certain there were no rustlers working in the area.

Dad was nearsighted, and when he forgot his glasses he had a difficult time spotting the cattle in the distance. Whenever he saw something that looked like a cow he would call me to his side and say, "Lowell, what do you see?" My eyes were young and strong, and I would tell Dad what I saw. Often what he thought were cows were only clumps of weeds and brush; but sometimes I found cattle that he had missed, standing in the shade of the trees in one of the distant coulees.

When it comes to heaven and eternity, most of us are so nearsighted we need someone with stronger spiritual eyes than we have or else a greater revelation of eternity to help us see what seems invisible. We not only have the testimony of the apostle John in the Book of Revelation, we have the experiences of many saints who have peered through the porthole of time into eternity.

When Thomas Edison, the famous scientist and inventor, lay dying he saw heaven, and he cried out, "It is very beautiful over there!" When evangelist Dwight L. Moody, the Billy Graham of his day, was dying he said, "I have been within the gates and seen the children, Dwight and Irene." Dwight and Irene were two of his grandchildren who had died years earlier.

General Booth, founder of the Salvation Army, had a vision of heaven and said he saw many angels and saints. He also described a celestial being, "human, yet angelic" in his beauty. He recognized this being as a friend who had died a number of years before.

Betty Malz, the wife of my associate evangelist Carl Malz, had the unusual experience of being dead for 28 minutes. The doctors and nurses were convinced she was dead and turned off the life-support system that had been maintaining her vital body functions. During her 28 minutes in eternity Betty saw sights that were breathtaking. When she returned to her body she reported, "As I looked inside the gates of heaven, as I stood there, I received something I can never explain. I shall never forget the majesty of the presence of God in heaven."

In the last chapter I mentioned some of the

wonderful dimensions of experience that we will enjoy in eternity, and there are many more!

We will enjoy new transportation! Here on Earth we have moved from travel by foot to travel by horse, to travel by train, to travel by supersonic spacecraft. Albert Einstein, the genius who developed the theory of relativity that gave birth to the atomic bomb, theorized about travel at the speed of light (186,000 miles per second). In eternity we will travel even faster. The expanse of space is so great that even at the speed of light we could not cover the universe as quickly as necessary; we will probably travel at the speed of thought!

Sadhu Singh, a Christian leader in India who died some years ago, had a vision of heaven. He said, "In heaven, distance is never felt by anyone, for as soon as one forms the wish to go to a certain place he at once finds himself there. Distances are felt only in the material world. If one wishes to see a saint in another sphere, whether he is transported there in a moment of thought or at once, the distant saint arrives in His presence."

Praise God! Travel at the speed of thought sounds fantastic to the mortal mind, but this will probably be the special dimension of travel we will experience in eternity.

We will enjoy special communications! Betty Malz tells that around the throne of God she saw peoples of many languages worshiping God. Although they spoke in different languages, each fully understood what the others were saying. Communication will be perfect because we will have complete understanding in eternity.

Daisy Dryden, a child whose predeceased brother often came to visit her while she lay on her deathbed, said, "We just talk with our think!" Imagine talking with your think. This will be a special experience in eternity.

We will enjoy worshiping God! Mankind has felt many consuming desires, but most of them have been destructive. Unbridled cravings for food, sex, liquor, other pleasures and power have always corrupted the persons driven by them. But there is a holy desire, a thirst for holy things that is divine and will be the ultimate experience. Jesus said, *"Blessed are they which do hunger and thirst after righteousness: for they shall be filled"* (Matthew 5:6).

The word *blessed* means *happy!* Jesus said

the individual who hungers and thirsts for God will be happy. Because we were created by God we have a craving for God. In eternity this spiritual craving will be experienced in its fullest measure through worship.

I know it is hard to imagine spending forever worshiping and serving God, but it is our limited flesh that causes us to think this way. To the sensualist, to spend eternity with thousands of the most beautiful women and enjoy their sexual favors sounds exciting. To the glutton, spending eternity with delightful foods sounds exciting. But to the Christian, spending eternity with God who is pure love and power will be the most exciting experience one could have.

The prophet Isaiah had a vision of the Lord of glory, and he reported, *"In the year that king Uzziah died I saw also the Lord sitting upon a throne, high and lifted up, and his train filled the temple. Above it stood the seraphims: each one had six wings; with (two) he covered his face, and with (two) he covered his feet, and with (two) he did fly. And one cried unto another, and said, Holy, holy, holy, is the Lord of hosts: the whole earth is full of his glory. And the posts of the door moved at* the voice of him that cried, and the house was filled with smoke" (Isaiah 6:1-4).

Here was Isaiah's reaction to this holy sight: *"Then said I, Woe is me! for I am undone; because I am a man of unclean lips, and I dwell in the midst of a people of unclean lips: for mine eyes have seen the King, the Lord of hosts. Then flew one of the seraphims unto me, having a live coal in his hand, which he had taken with the tongs from off the altar: and he laid it upon my mouth, and said, Lo, this hath touched thy lips; and thine iniquity is taken away, and thy sin purged.*

"Also I heard the voice of the Lord, saying, Whom shall I send, and who will go for us? Then said I, Here am I; send me" (Isaiah 6:5-8).

As soon as Isaiah saw the Lord he was changed from a self-righteous prophet into a man desperate for spiritual cleansing. This is the beauty of worshiping God: it transforms us from sinners into saints. After Moses worshiped God on the Mount of the Law and returned to the people, his face shone with such glory that they had to put a veil over his face to keep its brightness from hurting their eyes. This is the radiance and glory that will result from our worship of God.

Many still wonder if God is on an ego trip because He desires our worship. Not at all! As a loving parent rejoices in the love of the child hugging him, so God rejoices in our love for Him. The more we worship God, the more God will bless us with a fuller revelation of Himself and the abundance of His love. God has devoted Himself to giving us everything He has; this is why the Bible says that we are *"heirs of God and joint heirs with Christ!"*

We will enjoy the communion of our loved ones and the saints of all the ages! How many loved ones do you have in heaven now—a mom or dad, husband or wife, brother or sister, son or daughter, a good friend? A few years ago I met an elderly Christian man who said, "Lowell, I have more loved ones waiting for me on the other side than I have friends on this side."

In eternity you will be reunited with all of those you love more than life itself. Can you imagine the joy of seeing your father and mother, young and in their prime, full of health and radiance? Just think of seeing that departed loved one who died as a child, full of life and youth, smiling and beckoning to you with outstretched arms. Oh, hallelujah, won't it be wonderful there!

I have a brother waiting for me. His name is Laverne. He was just a baby when he left this world, about 1 year old. He used to jump up and down in his crib while I played my guitar for him and sang. I have two godly grandmothers waiting for me. They prayed that the Lundstrom family would come to Jesus Christ and be saved. I have a multitude of friends waiting for me—and so do you!

I can't think of a greater way to spend eternity than enjoying the fellowship of friends and loved ones. There is hope! There is a tomorrow! There is a future! There is a new world coming! God said, *"Behold, I make all things new!"*

Closing Comments

I hope you are certain about where you will spend eternity. If you have any doubt as to whether or not you will make it to heaven, you should pray—NOW! Receive Jesus Christ as your personal Savior! Ask Him to come into your heart and life and save you from your sins.

There is too much at stake to delay in making your decision.

Yesterday is in the tomb of time...
Tomorrow is in the womb of time...
TODAY IS ALL YOU'VE GOT!

Receiving Jesus Christ is the most important decision you will ever make. It is as simple as a-b-c:

a. Acknowledge you have sinned and failed God.

b. Believe that Jesus Christ died for your sins and rose again.

c. Commit your life to Him fully and obey His Holy Word.

Pray this prayer meaningfully, from the depth of your heart:

Lord Jesus, I believe you died for my sins, and I admit I have sinned against you. I receive you now into my heart as my Savior. Forgive me and restore me to God's favor. I know you bled and died for my transgressions, and I believe you rose from the dead.

If you prayed this prayer sincerely, the same wind of the Holy Spirit that has been whispering, "Warning!" is now whispering, "Peace! All is well."

I would like to hear from you if you have

made a personal decision to follow Jesus Christ. Write to me and you will receive a personal reply:

LOWELL LUNDSTROM
Sisseton, South Dakota 57262

In Canada write:

LOWELL LUNDSTROM
Box 4000
Winnipeg, Manitoba R3C 3W1

Thanks for sharing this moment with me!